Bronzer Alert

an essay

Vessa Yankevich

ISBN: 1497426901
ISBN-13: 978-1497426900

DEDICATION

MICHAEL SCHAAB

BRONZER ALERT

ACKNOWLEDGMENTS

Thanks Dave Newman for pushing me to write, friends for encouraging me to write this, Zach Bukowski for getting me drunk and helping me to deal with this. Love you all!

BRONZER ALERT

By VESSA YANKEVICH

BRONZER ALERT

Ted calls from rehab and tells me he needs to go to the hospital. The voices are getting louder and they are telling him to jump off the Liberty Bridge. He thinks he might do it.

I'm sitting in the office with a to-do list and service plans I have no time to work on. I sigh away from the phone and put on my clinical voice and say, "Wow, Ted, how long have you been hearing the voices?"

Ted breathes heavy with his smoker lungs and says, "Umm, about two days."

"Ted, do you have a plan to end your life?"

"Yeah, I wanna jump off the bridge,

that's what they're telling me to do."

I feel I should ask a lot of questions, so when I tell my supervisor I'm going to the emergency room with Ted, he'll have complete confidence I've assessed Ted properly.

"Ted, so you are feeling suicidal. And what do you want the emergency room to help you with?"

I always feel awkward asking suicidal assessment questions.

Ted says, "I want them to adjust my meds so the voices will stop and I can sleep."

I lose my clinical voice and say, "When are you seeing your psychiatrist next?"

"Ahh, I think on Wednesday, but the voices are just too bad. I think I need to go to the hospital."

Ted says this like he's been practicing.

"Okay Ted, I'm going to talk to my supervisor. I'll be there in twenty minutes."

My job feels endless and the paperwork piles up. I imagine myself swimming through it, drowning. I die from paper suffocation. My punishment is being reincarnated as a schizophrenic, aimlessly roaming earth, hearing all the voices of my patients.

"Help me," a frustrated voice says. "Where are my bus tickets," a bossy voice shouts.

And, "I'm homeless."

And, "I have no money."

And, "I want to die."

The voices blend together, then I shoot myself.

Ted says, "Yeah, I talked with Jim and Kim and they think I should go since I haven't been able to sleep in three days."

I tell him his counselors and I will discuss his need to be re-evaluated.

I sigh and crack my neck. I feel a release of tension as I call my first morning appointment and tell her I can't make it.

"But Vessa, when am I going to see you?" she whines in her high voice, like we don't see each other weekly.

I say, "Don't worry Marsha, I'll see you next week."

She says, "But Vessa, I really need to talk to you about my voices."

I look down at my phone planner and say, "How about Thursday at 10 AM?"

"Oh, I have to pay my rent that day," she sighs.

"Okay, I'm open Friday at 2."

"Okay Vessa, I think I can do that. Meet me at the Bottom Dollar."

It's like talking to a child who was told no then yes.

"I can't wait to tell you about the food bank and all the nice things I got," she says.

"I can't wait either, Marsha," I say in an excited voice that matches hers.

"Vessa, I can't wait to see you. Oh, I can't wait!"

Marsha likes Bottom Dollar because the colors make her happy and it's bright inside and her voices don't go there. I think about how the bright aisles and warm color scheme work on her and everyone else. Marsha used to meet me at the Dunkin' Donuts but became scared of the place when two little girls were there, shouting and laughing.

"Vessa, can you stop them? It's too loud," Marsha said. She looked frightened and put on her headphones to play static. Marsha likes the sound of white noise. She says it keeps the voices in the other realm.

Marsha looked at me with her taped-up headphones. "Vessa, they keep looking at me. They think I'm bad."

I looked at the kids munching away on their donuts and their chocolate covered faces.

I said, "Marsha, they're just eating their donuts."

Marsha said, "I don't like children, they're loud, it scares me."

She looked scared and not because it's uncool to like children, but because the sound of them is too strong for her. I smiled at her softly.

I said, "They won't bother you."

Marsha said, "But Vessa, why are they laughing like that?"

I said, "They're just having fun."

Marsha said, "I don't know. They are so loud."

I said, "Marsha, what helps you when you get stressed?"

Marsha was unaware of her own paranoia. I could have explained it, but this is her reality and she would not understand.

Marsha perked up like the kids had vanished and said, "Well Vessa, I like to listen to my sound machine and the sounds on the TV. It sounds like the ocean in a seashell. I go for walks with my sound machine and I clean my apartment with it. It was only five dollars at the Family Dollar."

I said, "Wow that's a good deal."

She said, "You think so, Vessa?"

I said, "Yeah, it sure is!"

When I look at Marsha and her beaming blue eyes, I sometimes imagine her as an angel floating up to the light she so often talks about when life is good to her.

~~~

I pack my car with my keys dangling from my mouth, my computer bag falling off my shoulder, my purse hanging from my neck, my agenda book tucked under one arm, and a bag of papers that clients need to sign spilling all over the parking lot.

I feel like mugger-bait waiting to be devoured. I climb into my car filled with empty fast food and coffee containers and turn the key three times. I pray, "Please Lord, not today," and the ignition clunkles and revs and works. I fist pump the air and yell, "Hallelujah!" I drive to the North Side and pass row houses and the boarded-up porn theater, now a historic landmark, painted with flowers where the windows are missing.

The North Side is home to wealthy urban professionals, crack addicts, and poor black families. I like seeing clients on the North Side because people look at you and ask how your day is. Nebby neighbors tell you if your patient is home or not and where your patient went and with whom.

People know their neighbors here.

I roll up to the rehab center, nestled between old factories and row houses. Old and young men stand outside smoking cheap rolled cigarettes.

One guy in a Steelers shirt smiles and says hi.

I say, "How are you?" in my social work voice.

He says, "Good," grinning at me like I'm naked.

He looks like he has lived two lives, mine and his both. We are around the same age. I imagine what he would have been like if his life had been different, if he'd had more opportunities or made different choices.

I go into the lobby and a woman on the phone points to the sign-in chart. I sign it and fill in the time and date.

"Hi!" I smile. "Can I please speak with Ted Williams?"

"Hold on," she says into the phone, then calls over the intercom, "Ted, can you please come down to the lobby?"

She gets back on the phone and says, "Girl, you will never guess what I made last night for supper."

I wonder what she made, and if her friend even cares.

"I made fried chicken, greens, and corn. Girl, it was the shit!"

She goes on about her special flouring and batter and seasonings. I think of what I will cook tonight after work.

"Excuse me," I say, "can you call Ted again?"

She looks over her plastic glasses and says, "Sure honey, just a minute."

She says, "Ted, can you come down to the lobby, *please*? Your social worker's here."

I wait five minutes and glance at my phone.

She looks up from her phone and says,

"He still hasn't come down here?"

She sighs, "Hold on, honey," to her friend and wobbles to the back. A minute later she reappears with Ted and sits back down at her desk.

Ted shuffles down the hall, yawning, Skittles in his hand.

"Hey Ted," I say, "How are you?"

He is smiling and tossing Skittles in his mouth. "Not good, mmm, not good at all. How are you, Miss Vessa? You want some Skittles?"

I say no, even though I'm really hungry and shaky from caffeine.

"I'm doing great!" I say with a big smile.

Ted makes *mmm* vocal tics, due to the side effects of taking first generation antipsychotics for years. We go into the office and the shelves are full of relapse-prevention worksheets and handbooks.

"I keep hearing these voices, *mmm*, and I can't sleep and I'm having suicidal thoughts."

Ted says this like he's reading a script for a play called *Get Out of Rehab*.

"What kind of thoughts?" I say. I use my clinical voice.

"To jump off a bridge. I need to go to

the hospital."

"Well, what hospital?" I say.

"I don't want to go to Mercy," Ted says. "The last time I went there they messed up my meds and the voices got worse."

He breathes heavy and coughs.

"Hey, we can always go to WPIC if you want," I say.

Most case managers hate WPIC (Western Psychiatric Institute and Clinic), but I love it because I get to sit on the internet and catch up on paperwork and talk to random psych patients and people coming off drugs.

WPIC is productive, sad, comical.

"Yeah, as long as they can adjust my meds and I can get some sleep."

I wonder again if Ted is really suicidal or if he just wants to leave rehab.

Ted is not like most crack addicts who take advantage of you by demanding you do things for them. When you say no, they avoid your calls and relapse. Sometimes you find them dead, sometimes you find them at the hospital, or in another state, or just avoiding you while you're calling their cell phones and pounding on their doors.

Ted is a tall, heavy black man in his

fifties who attends church every Sunday and helps his pastor with lawn work and fixing cars.

Ted went to rehab after being clean nine months following 20 years of straight crack smoking. I wanted to believe it was me, that I was a great case manager and he was a miracle addict who could just stop one day and not relapse. The reality was that in those nine months, he had stable housing, was living with his mom, and religiously attending NA meetings.

That probably explained things.

Two months ago, Ted told me Little Freddy down the street would stop him while he was walking his nephew to school.

Little Freddy would say, "Hey brother, did you get your check? Wanna smoke, brother? I can get you some good, good crack."

And Ted would say, "No, I can't," and look down and walk on with his nephew.

His 10-year-old nephew had to be walked to school because otherwise he would skip school and hang out with the kids that liked to cut up and hang outside the Y. Ted said his nephew's mom turned tricks for crack and his dad was in prison.

Ted told me that, when he was walking his nephew to school one day, Little Freddy popped out on the street corner and asked him if he wanted to smoke. Ted said his mom was screaming at him a lot and wanted him to watch his nephew too much and he gave up.

Ted went to the convenience store with Little Freddy, cashed his SSI check and bought $600 worth of crack. They had a ball for a week, then they got $300 more on an IOU from their dealer, who owned a gun and came looking for them, and Ted ran away and hid in the trash.

Ted said his voices were really bad and he thought he was going to kill himself by jumping off the Liberty Bridge, so he showed up at the hospital.

Ted always picks the Liberty Bridge even though he lives closer to other, more convenient bridges.

At the hospital, Ted's eyes looked big and tired and glassy. He laid on the bed with the hospital cover over him and said he wanted to go to rehab.

Ted knows the right things to say. If you say you're suicidal and you have a plan, you become a top priority. It's an automatic ticket into the hospital. If you say you're homeless and coming down off a drug, you get booted or withdraw in the waiting room.

I can't drive Ted in my car because of insurance liability, ever since someone attacked their case manager while driving to an appointment. It made the paper and WPIC got stricter and made it harder for case workers to help people.

Right now we wait in the office, Ted and me. Ted wants to use my work phone to make plans and call his insurance company and his mom. I let him use it and we wait.

I look at my personal phone and text Zane, the guy I'm seeing. He texts me all the time and is attentive. I met him through his best friend, who I used to sleep with.

One night I met up with Zane and some friends at a dive bar. We got wasted on dollar PBRs and he followed me home. We made out in alleyways and against cemetery walls and fences. He stuck his hands between my tights and said, "Can we just get naked?"

I told him we shouldn't have sex, then

I said we should have sex, then we had sex.

I woke up and my head hurt and he was in my bed, naked.

I look up at Ted to see he is not looking. I text Zane: let's hang out later, smiley face, smiley face, exclamation point! I look up at Ted to make sure he doesn't notice and toss my phone into my purse.

The ambulance arrives, and a man and woman walk into the office with a drug counselor. Ted tells them straight-up that he is hearing voices and has suicidal thoughts. They ask him what hospital he wants to go to and he says, "WPIC, please."

They walk him to the ambulance and he climbs in.

I wave and shout, "I'll see you there."

Ted doesn't notice.

I walk to my car and check my phone. Zane texts back that he can see me after band practice.

I text: ok cool.

I climb into my car and gulp down some coffee.

I park in the back parking lot of WPIC after I flash my ID to the security guard. I look at my phone and Zane texts me about drinking beers with his band members after practice.

I text: ok cool rock on drinky drinky.

I think about how corny that sounds and erase it.

I text: sounds fun, and toss my phone on the passenger seat.

I swipe my ID into the security scanner. The doors open, I go down the elevator, and make my way through the maze of the first floor. I pound on the emergency room door and the woman who checks people in looks at me then looks down at the computer and continues to type. I wait. I knock again and she looks up and sighs, then comes to the door and opens it. I walk in and the security guard looks at me like I'm a terrorist who just walked in with bombs strapped to my tits. I look at him and flash my ID.

"You need to be searched, it's policy."

"But I work for WPIC."

"But you don't work in the DEC."

"I'm here with a patient."

"But you don't. Work. In the DEC."

I want to flip him the bird and tell him how sad it must have been to not make the cut for the police force and have to settle for life as a security guard.

He comes over with his wand, tells me to put my arms out, and wands me. He asks for my purse and his buzzed head snoops through it. He hands it back with a serious face and says, "I need to see your computer," and I hand him the bag.

He opens it and closes it and says, "Here you go, you can go now." I ask him if he can let me into the back room. He quietly walks to the door and unlocks it, scowling.

I run to the back desk and my computer bag falls off. I put it back over my shoulder and walk to the back. Ted is there and the EMTs are gone.

"Hey Miss Vessa."

"Hey buddy, you got here before me," I say in a happy tone.

Ted walks over to the TV and sits next to a woman wrapped in a hospital sheet. She's coming off of heroin. She stares at the screen and shakes. I go behind the desk, plop my laptop, open up PSYCHCONSULT and work on a service plan. Then I work on my notes, read my e-mails, and work on another service plan.

Ted walks up and I smile.

"Mmm, how much longer?"

"It seems busy. I'll go ask when a clinician will see you."

I turn and open the back door. Doctors, clinicians, and social workers type on computers. Some are on phones talking to other social workers from other hospitals about open beds, rejections. I walk in, look at the screen, count the people ahead of Ted, and ask when a clinician can see him.

The nurse glares at me, says, "We will see him when we can," and rushes out of the room.

I wave at the clinicians and say, "I'm with Ted. If you need me, I'll be in the waiting room, on my computer."

No one looks up from the screens and I walk out and sit down. Ted is standing behind the counter. I say, "There are four more people ahead of you, and then a clinician can see you."

Ted says okay and I ask him if he wants anything to snack on. He says yes and I grab him a turkey cheese sandwich from the pink bin and hand it to him. He walks over to the TV, sits down, and eats.

An autistic teenager with short hair crawls on the floor, screams, and pulls on

25

her shirt like it's on fire. Her parents walk next to her. They look exhausted and worried. A guy walks back and forth and sees me looking and starts to meow. I smile and he meows, then roars, and then licks his wrist. I look down and he walks over to me and asks if I can take him out to smoke. I tell him I don't work in the DEC, that I'm a case manager in the community.

He says, "Goddamn it," and roars like a lion in heat.

I apologize and stare at him with a concerned look and say, "Hey man, if I could, I would take you out for a smoke."

He looks over the counter into the pink bin and says, "What's that stuff?"

"Graham crackers and turkey sandwiches. Would you like one?"

"Yeah."

I hand him some graham crackers and a turkey sandwich. I ask him where he's from. He says McKeesport. I ask him what he's here for and he says he's pissed and angry and doesn't give a fuck. He bites into his sandwich and half of it vanishes into his mouth. He looks at me for a bit and I look at him.

"Can I use the phone?" he mumbles

with a mouth full of food.

"Sure, it's for everyone. You don't have to ask."

He tries calling out and slams his fist against the receiver. "Fucking goddam it!"

"What's wrong?"

"It won't go through."

"You have to dial nine first."

He glances at me and says, "Oh."

He talks like he's screaming, mostly about how he will quit and how he wants to come home. I hear a loud woman on the other line. I hear him crying and I start typing up a note for billable. He walks across the floor and screams, "Motherfuckin' bitch!" Then he sits down, eats graham crackers and watches the TV.

I go on Facebook and read posts about people's problems, their bands, their awesome boyfriends they love so much, their bowel movements, cut-and-pasted inspirational quotes with the ocean in the background.

Then I hear shouting and screaming coming from the front of the emergency room. The door bursts open. A thin middle-aged woman and a man run through the door and I hear the woman shout, "I've been shot! I've been shot!"

Blood runs down her face, all over her shirt. I assume the man and woman have gotten into a domestic dispute and he shot her. Blood is on his leg. He runs around and screams, "Get down, get down!"

My father killed my pet chicken when he started to think he was god after my mother died from a brain tumor.

I think about this and I stare at these people and try to make sense of what is happening.

The woman runs around shouting, "I've been shot," and the man keeps screaming, too. A herd of people from the front room run in, screaming. Someone else shouts, "There's a shooter, get down!" People are diving to the floor and scurrying behind chairs.

I think about cockroaches scurrying around when the light turns on. I watch everyone over the desk. Ted runs into an evaluation room. I get down behind the desk and people are still shouting, "Get down, there's a shooter." They are screaming. Their voices sound like burning snakes, shrill and frightened.

I think of the time my foster parents

made me kill the garter snakes and burn them to ward off evil. I can't move. Nurses and doctors run past me into the back room with their computers. I feel like I should follow Ted and try to keep him calm, but I'm paralyzed, that scared.

I got into social work because my heart seemed unfit to do anything else. My life was social work. I moved from foster home to foster home wanting to be loved by someone.

Instead I was abused. I ran away. I got sent to a girls home.

Now I crawl to the back room, where nurses and doctors and clients are balled on the floor. Everyone tries to make sense of what is happening.

A frantic bubble-eyed nurse shouts, "Call 911!"

A nerdy-looking psychiatrist with big glasses and a bowl cut calls 911.

The nurses' aide in bright pink Breast Cancer Awareness scrubs clings to her Louis Vuitton purse. She chokes for air and cries. "There are shooters and they were shooting at me," she says.

Another nurse bawls, "I saw him, I saw him!" She's hyperventilating and bawling.

Everyone is low, crouched behind or against something or in a corner, in the fetal position, praying or screaming or whispering.

A couple and their son, who look like they just stepped out of a J. Crew ad, are against the wall. The son is engrossed in his Gameboy. He doesn't look bothered or phased.

I cling to the edge of a desk. I think of a survival tactic, plan for all of us to run out the ambulance entrance if a shooter comes in. Then I second-guess myself.

I wonder how others would react if I just ran out the door.

Maybe they'd think I was the shooter. Maybe they'd shoot me. I don't want to die or scare people, so I stay put and avoid my intruding thoughts.

I crawl over to the frantic nurse. I feel her body heat and sweat penetrate from her as I rub her back softly. I tell her it's okay. A young and fit intern doctor crawls over and takes charge. I figure since she's a doctor she must be good at this, so I go back to my position under the desk.

The doctor stiffly pats the nurse's back

and demands, "Now look at me, look at me. I need you to breathe. Can you breathe for me?"

I think this sounds forced, like the doctor's reading out of a manual for calming a person down.

Who says a thing like that? Who says "breathe for me" and means it?

The doctor holds the shocked nurse's shoulders and insists, "Everything will be okay, just breathe with me and count to ten. Are you ready? One, breathe, two, breathe..."

The doctor counts and breathes like she's a yoga instructor, trying to convince herself and everyone else that she's in control.

The nurse screams, "I have asthma, I can't breathe!" She digs through her purse and wheezes, "I can't breathe, oh Lord help me, I can't breathe! He tried to kill me. He tried to kill me!"

"Where is your inhaler?" the doctor asks slowly.

The nurse pulls it out of her purse and puffs on it, but continues to cry and hyperventilate. The doctor sits up straight and crawls away, while the nurse goes on breathing, back against the wall.

The rest of us watch the surveillance screen. A frantic nurse shouts, "Another shooter is coming through the door!" and screams.

Another nurse screams and watches the surveillance screen, "He went out of the building. I saw him leave, I saw him."

The screams ricochet through the waiting room. The frantic woman who was shot at shouts, "He's in here, he has a key!"

Everyone curls up tight. I cling to the desk like it's a protective shield. The nurse with the inhaler is crying and we are all quiet, too afraid to move.

A nerdy bowl-cut psychiatrist talks to 911 and says there are shooters and that we need an ambulance at the DEC. Two people have been shot. He talks to a cop and relays the reports of frantic people.

The mechanical doctor calmly tells everyone to stay down. He says there is more than one shooter. Time seems still and surreal.

I pull out my work phone and text my boss: there is a shooter at the hospital. He texts me back: confused. I text him: there is someone at WPIC shooting people. I feel strange texting my boss, like I shouldn't be. Like texting is wrong, ridiculous. Like I should be frantic and too scared to do anything but run around screaming. But I feel I should let my boss know, let someone I know, know.

I hear the Bronzer Alert go off and the mechanical doctor tell people to remain on the floor. The nerdy psychiatrist reports that the cops got the shooter. The oblivious boy continues to play his Gameboy, as his parents hold him close. I try to make sense of what's happening and ask the doctor if the shooter is dead.

The J. Crew father with his slick haircut glares at me and says with conviction, "There is a child in here." The boy is lost in his Gameboy. The mom covers his ears. The doctor turns to me and whispers, "Yes."

A nurse comes through the side door with the bleeding woman and man. I see bloody towels fall on the floor and then I hear the EMTs talking to the doctors. They get the man and woman strapped to a bed and rush them out the ambulance entrance.

ABOUT THE AUTHOR

Vessa Yankevich lives in Pittsburgh, PA, in the vibrant neighborhood of Lawrenceville, where she works as a social worker.

44588709R00021

Made in the USA
Columbia, SC
19 December 2018